Lindbergh
Looks Back

LINDBERGH
LOOKS BACK

A BOYHOOD REMINISCENCE

CHARLES A.
LINDBERGH

Foreword by **Reeve Lindbergh**

Introduction by Brian Horrigan

MINNESOTA HISTORICAL SOCIETY PRESS

Published in 2002 by the Minnesota Historical Society Press, St. Paul

This book, first published in 1972 by the Minnesota Historical Society under the title *Boyhood on the Upper Mississippi: A Reminiscent Letter*, contains a new foreword by Reeve Lindbergh adapted from her book *Under a Wing: A Memoir.* Reprinted with permission of Simon & Schuster from UNDER A WING: *A Memoir* by Reeve Lindbergh. Copyright © 1998 by Reeve Lindbergh.

www.mnhs.org/mhspress

International Standard Book Number: 0-87351-422-X

Manufactured in Canada
10 · 9   8   7   6   5   4   3   2

♾ The paper used in this publication meets the minimum requirements of the American National Standard for Information Sciences–Permanence for Printed Library Materials, ANSI Z39.48–1984.

A Cataloging-in-Publication record for this book is available from the Library of Congress.

The Minnesota Historical Society Press gratefully acknowledges the assistance of society staff members Paul Blankman, Brian Horrigan, William (Bill) Johnson, Eric Mortenson, Claudia Nicholson, and Bridget White with this publication.

MY FATHER has been dead for more than a quarter of a century now, but I still miss him, and I expect I always will. Still, whenever I want to find him again, I travel to Minnesota to visit his boyhood home, the Lindbergh house and farm in Little Falls. I do this even though the Lindbergh home in Little Falls is an odd place for me to look for my father. Since 1931 it has belonged to the state of Minnesota and not to my family at all. Furthermore, the Lindbergh family life that took place there, day to day, has nothing to do with my childhood or my adult life, and dates back to the years before 1920, a time even more distant to my family than the flight of the *Spirit of St. Louis.*

Like the aircraft hanging in the great gallery of the Smithsonian Air and Space Museum, the house in Little Falls seems an artifact of our family's pioneer days, a vestige of such unfamiliar and ancient times that to present-day Lindbergh children, and grandchildren, and great-grandchildren, it might just as well be a covered wagon.

Why does this place speak so strongly to me? I never went to Little Falls with my father, and was not even fully aware of how much it meant to him until a year or two before his death. He occasionally talked about, but never personally introduced me to, the old house on the bank of the upper Mississippi, with its wood-

REEVE LINDBERGH, youngest child of Charles A. Lindbergh and Anne Morrow Lindbergh, is the author of numerous books, including *Under a Wing: A Memoir.*

THE RESTORED CHARLES A. LINDBERGH HOUSE in Charles A. Lindbergh State Park on the upper Mississippi River near Little Falls, Minnesota, in 1971

burning cookstove and its glassed-in china cabinets and its steep stairs. He mentioned once or twice in passing, but never showed me directly, the wide, screened porch overlooking the riverbank where as a boy he kept a cot and blankets, summer and winter, because whenever he got the chance, he liked to sleep at least halfway outdoors. If I close my eyes today I can see him there, on his cot, stretching out to his full length in contentment, a young, long, lean boy, on a farm by a river, in 1918, with his dog, Wahgoosh, curled up at his feet.

Now that I know the house and farm, and have been there many times, I think I know the boy and his dog, too, breathing quietly in each other's presence, eyes open, listening for a long time in the dark before sleep comes over either one of them, hearing together the night sounds of the farm, and the comforting creak and settle of the house beside them, and the wet, whispered running of the river, the young, long, lean Mississippi River, in the headlong inevitable rush of its own Minnesota beginnings, running by. I like knowing that my father slept with the Mississippi River running right by him where he lay, on its way from the swimming holes and berry bushes of Little Falls to a destiny of faraway grandeurs and immensities, flowing first to Minneapolis and St. Paul, and then to Dubuque, and Hannibal, and St. Louis, and Memphis, and Baton Rouge, and finally all the way out to spill itself completely into the Gulf of Mexico.

My father, too, had come such a long way from his beginnings that it took time to reestablish him in my imagination here, in Minnesota, in his early home. It was a hard task, but a familiar one, to reclaim him from his own history and make him mine. This effort in itself causes one of the strangest interminglings I have come to know as the child of famous parents: the give-and-take between public impression and private memory, each informing, educating, correcting, and ultimately humanizing the other, over time. It is an important effort, however odd or uncomfortable it sometimes feels. I have learned that by pursuing my own history consistently, pursuing it with compassion and without fear, I will discover over and over again that the people I love best can never be lost to me, after all.

I did not even know, until my father began to be so busy about it in the 1960s, that the old farm still existed, not just a memory but a real place that I could someday visit. All the stories my father told about the farm during my earlier childhood were so deeply embedded in the past that there seemed no

CHARLES and Wahgoosh, 1918

possibility of a present-day connection. I knew only that before I was born, before the Second World War, before the flight to Paris, before the *First* World War, before my father had an airplane to fly or even a car to drive, he was a boy on a farm in Minnesota. I understood that this part of his life took place long, long before my time, in the era that my sister and I called "The Olden Days." I felt that it was far out of my reach geographically, too, set in a part of the country known to my New England mind as "Way out West."

I do remember my father telling us how cold the winters were in central Minnesota when he was a boy, how deep and quiet and all-encompassing the snows. I remember hearing about the lilac and honeysuckle bushes his mother planted along the road in front of her house, and how good the sweet corn tasted that grew in Morrison County in the summer, better than anywhere else in the world.

I can't answer the questions I wanted to ask my father when I first visited his home in Minnesota, but I have come back again and again, carrying with me what I already knew of him, bringing away what I did not.

I know that my father was a good boy, growing up in Minnesota, and that he grew into a good man. He was a man who continued to grow, along with his own century, through aviation and technology and war and peace and family life, and love. When he said late in life, "If I had to choose, I'd rather have birds than airplanes," he did not believe that he really had to choose, or that the world really had to choose, but he knew that there was much work ahead for him, and for us all, if birds and airplanes were to coexist in harmony far into the technological future.

He was a man who loved his family and who loved his country, too, in a way that seems old-fashioned to many people now, but that comes naturally enough to those who know the country very well from earliest childhood, with a physical as well as an emotional understanding. When his life became more complicated than he ever had wished it or expected it to be, he was able to reach back to that understanding, to an affection for the earth he had known and experienced in his childhood, combined with a never-ending fascination for the land he had flown over as a young pilot, and the world he came to know internationally, as an older pilot. This love for the living earth, and for life itself, was his earliest strength, second only to his association with my mother in its intensity, and strong enough that it sustained him all the way through the very last days of his life.

I have never gotten over my original feeling that in Minnesota, all the elements in my father are finally brought together, and that here, if I can only pay close enough attention, he will be fully restored

to me, time and time again. Everything is there: the childhood and the farm, the birds and the airplanes, the marriage, the war, the family, the conservation work, and the final days in Maui. Here, ever more open to my understanding as I make room to accommodate them, are gathered in one place both the simple truths and the complicated ones, each well grounded in the real life of a boy in the early 1900s, in the work and the rhythms of a farm, and in the long, strong running of a great American river, always growing wider, and flowing deeper, as it finds its way from town to town and farm to farm, always moving steadily toward the ocean.

Brian Horrigan

This is to be an autobiography. I have long intended to write a record of my life . . .
to make an attempt to set down my own character and actions in my own manner
and through my own mind and pen. I am looking forward with anticipation to living
again the years of my childhood; meeting again friends who are dead, others whom
I have forgotten as time has drifted in between us. I shall hunt partridges with my
father in Minnesota, suffer through the hours in school in Washington, farm again
on the banks of the Mississippi.

WITH THESE WORDS, Charles Lindbergh penned a first few, highly self-conscious pages of boyhood memoir, and then ceremoniously transcribed the draft into a gilt-edged blank book. He was living in Paris with his wife and two small sons; it was December 1938, and he was just thirty-six years old. Lindbergh recognized that he was starting his life review at an unusually early stage. He knew that if he waited until he was older, "possibly the story would be better told . . . but then I may never reach forty or fifty and it might not be told at all. Besides, it can always be rewritten." [1]

Lindbergh did rewrite that story, many times. In fact, by 1938, he had already published one of the best-selling autobiographies in

BRIAN HORRIGAN, exhibit curator at the Minnesota Historical Society, researched and wrote the text for the revised exhibits at the Charles A. Lindbergh House historic site in Little Falls, Minnesota.

American history (though it contained few boyhood adventures). But in the 1930s, when he opened the floodgate of memory, a river coursed through it, one that did not stop flowing until his death. Lindbergh was a tireless creator and jealous guardian of his own life story. Six of the seven books that bear his name are autobiographical.[2] From his famous New York–to–Paris flight in 1927 to the end of his life—a span of nearly fifty years—Lindbergh turned repeatedly to life-writing. His autobiographical works form a remarkably diverse collection: an immediate recounting by a young and instant celebrity of the first nonstop, solo flight across the Atlantic Ocean; a thousand-page gathering of wartime journals; a troubled and ruminative postwar essay; a brilliant retelling of the story of the most famous flight of the century, interwoven with memoir; a summing-up of a lifetime of "values"; and a lengthy letter, about his Minnesota boyhood, that became *Lindbergh Looks Back*.

SELF-DOCUMENTATION seems to have been second nature to Lindbergh. As a boy he had occasionally kept a journal—during a 1915 boat trip down the Mississippi River with his father, for example, and on some of his motorcycle trips after high school. Lindbergh was an inveterate compiler of exhaustive lists, such as one documenting all the trips he had made in his youth, which he then recorded—color-coded by type of conveyance—on a huge map of the United States. He often brought a camera along on his trips (even taking pictures while parachuting) and mounted his snapshots into neat albums. His "recording" personality served him well when he began his career as a pilot, always making time to keep careful logs of his all of his flights.

Written in 1927 in the frenzied wake of the transatlantic flight, *"We"* was Lindbergh's baptism in the fire of autobiography. The aviator had signed a contract to tell his story, but when the publisher presented him with a ghostwritten version, he rejected it and promised to deliver his own manuscript in three weeks. *"We"* is short on childhood detail and almost entirely devoid of emotion and personal reflection. A good deal of time is given to tales from Lindbergh's days on the barnstorming circuit, in air cadet training, and flying the airmail. The entire New York–to–Paris flight is dispatched in just seven pages! None of this mattered, of course, as the book went on to become one of the best-selling titles of the 1920s.[3]

After *"We,"* Lindbergh did not write another word of memoir for more than a decade, with an important exception. In the early 1930s, he began a correspondence with a curator at the Minnesota Historical Society, Grace Lee Nute, who was doing research for a biography of Charles A. Lindbergh, Sr., the aviator's Congressman father. At great length and during a period of more than ten years, Lindbergh wrote letters to Nute that, in fact, constitute the earliest versions of the childhood memories that he would revisit again and again over the next fifty years. Thinking and writing about his father for Nute's project seem to have been a catalyst for Lindbergh to turn the biographical mirror toward himself.[4]

In the late 1930s, Lindbergh started earnestly keeping a journal. Living in Europe, and witnessing the gathering clouds of war, he realized "that I was taking part in one of the great crises of world history" and there were thus many developments that "were bound to make a journal well worth keeping."[5] This is classic understatement. During the years covered in his journal—1938 to 1945—Lindbergh was again in the public spotlight, first for his outspoken prewar warnings about Germany's military strength, then for his opposition to American entry into the war, and finally for his aerial combat activity (though as a civilian) in the South Pacific theater of war in 1944. In the late 1960s, Lindbergh was persuaded by his friend William Jovanovich to prepare the journals for publication. When the original handwritten journals were transcribed, they totaled more than three thousand typewritten pages. Cut by more than a third, *Wartime Journals*, in its published form is still a thousand pages long.

In 1948 Lindbergh returned again to the public eye with the phenomenally popular *Of Flight and Life*. Although not a memoir as such, *Of Flight and Life* in fewer than sixty printed pages finds Lindbergh in high autobiographical mode, dramatically retelling stories of a life-threatening moment in a test plane, an aerial combat mission, and a tour of the devastated ruins of post–World War II Germany. In the controversial second part of the book, Lindbergh issues a passionate jeremiad on the prospect of an "Atomic Age war" and the potential collapse of western civilization and spiritual values—and, surprisingly, makes something of a confession: "Like most of modern youth, I worshipped science. I was awed by its knowledge. . . . Now, I have lived to experience the early results of scientific materialism. . . . I have seen the science I worshipped, and the aircraft I loved, destroying the civilization I expected them to serve, and which I thought as permanent as earth itself."[6]

In the preface to his best-known book, Lindbergh calls *The Spirit of St. Louis* a "book about flying, and an aviator's life." It is certainly that, and more. He began writing this American epic in 1938, and worked on it during the next fourteen years. Originally, it seems, he envisioned his story of the flight as one component of a larger autobiography. Soon that story occupied center stage, and the book developed into two major parts—the first a tightly compressed retelling, much of it in dialogue, of the events leading up to the takeoff from New York; and the second, much larger part, an hour-by-hour account of the transatlantic flight, ending with the landing in Paris on the night of May 21, 1927. Working on his manuscript in 1944, Lindbergh began to layer his gripping story of the flight with "flashbacks," in almost cinematic style. As the weary flyer fights the urge to sleep and navigates his tiny plane through thunderclouds and icy rain, he lets his mind wander through the past, to his childhood in Minnesota and Detroit and Washington, D.C., and to his knockabout days as a barnstormer and air cadet. At a later stage in writing the book, Lindbergh changed every sentence in the manuscript to the present tense, which lent an immediacy and surprising forward momentum to the story. Readers—nearly every one of them familiar with the saga—found themselves racing through the book to see how it ended. Brilliantly innovative in structure and style, *The Spirit of St. Louis* was widely hailed as a magnificent literary achievement upon publication in 1953, and was awarded the Pulitzer Prize for biography in 1954.[7]

Even while working on the manuscript that became *The Spirit of St. Louis*, Lindbergh continued to revisit regions of his memory, in page after minutely handwritten page, day after day. The tentative title of this large-scale autobiographical work shifted during the years from "Forms" to "Limits of Knowledge" and "What Man Will

Make." It was never completed. Lindbergh knew he was dying in August 1974 when he turned over to William Jovanovich more than a thousand typewritten manuscript pages of this work, and nearly as many pages of related notes. Working with Yale University archivist Judith A. Schiff, Jovanovich shaped the manuscript into *Autobiography of Values*, Lindbergh's last work, published posthumously in 1978.

Autobiography of Values was never meant to be conventional autobiography. The book contains deeply personal strands woven through passionate reveries on mortality, reincarnation, and the nature of being. Lindbergh writes of scattering his father's cremated remains from an airplane: "Death transferred him from life back into matter. . . . I sense himself in me. . . . There are times when my reactions are identical with my memory of his—as though I actually were my father remembering the past, continuing in life beyond my death." [8]

Especially toward the end of his life, Lindbergh extended his autobiographical "project" into other areas. Beginning in 1968, he wrote extensive, line-by-line refutations of several biographies about himself, filing copies of these commentaries with a number of archives. He also carried on extensive correspondence with a handful of approved historians working on aspects of his life. Finally, when he was in his mid-sixties, Lindbergh reestablished a relationship with his fondly remembered boyhood home on the banks of the Mississippi and assisted the Minnesota Historical Society in developing an interpretive program at the former family farm in Little Falls.

Donated by the Lindbergh family to the state of Minnesota in memory of Lindbergh's father and namesake, the Little Falls property had been established in 1931 as Charles A. Lindbergh State Park. In 1969 the state transferred to the Minnesota Historical Society the administration of the house and seventeen surrounding acres. The society, after restoring them to the condition in which they had been during the family's residence there from 1906 to 1920, now operates the house and its grounds as a historic site open to the public. Lindbergh visited the site at least seven times between 1966 and 1973. He made audio recordings of several passages from

The Spirit of St. Louis for use in exhibits at the site and offered advice on a concept outline for the original exhibits in its visitor center, which he helped to dedicate in 1973.

Lindbergh also assisted with the restoration by writing a long letter about his early years to the society's director at the time, Russell W. Fridley. Composed in odd moments from October 1969 to February 1970, and mailed in several installments as Lindbergh traveled from the Philippines to Hong Kong to Europe to New York City, the letter proved to be of such historical interest and value that the society published it in 1972 under the title *Boyhood on the Upper Mississippi: A Reminiscent Letter.* In commemoration of the seventy-fifth anniversary of Lindbergh's flight across the Atlantic Ocean in 1927 and the one-hundredth anniversary of his birth in 1902, the book has now been reissued as *Lindbergh Looks Back: A Boyhood Reminiscence.*

Lindbergh's cooperation with the society was an altogether extraordinary relationship between a historical organization and a living figure stepping out of the pages of history. At its best, a historic house dedicated to interpreting the life of an individual is a biography in space, structure, and landscape. With Lindbergh's assistance, the house in Little Falls became more intimate and revealing—a boyhood story in three-dimensions.[9]

When Lindbergh began writing autobiography in 1938, he said he wanted "to make an attempt to set down my own character and actions in my own manner and through my own mind and pen." During his lifetime, Lindbergh felt compelled to be his own chronicler. No one else, he felt, had a greater right to tell the tale. On the strength of the stories contained here in *Lindbergh Looks Back*—and in his other enduring works of memory—it is clear that no one else knew the story as well as he did.

---

1. Unpublished fragment, Series V, Charles A. Lindbergh Papers, Manuscripts and Archives, Yale University Library.
2. The exception is *The Culture of Organs* (New York: P. B. Hoeber, 1938), which Lindbergh coauthored with Alexis Carrel, who had received a Nobel Prize in 1912 for his work on vascular suture and the transplantation of blood vessels and organs.

3. *"We": The Famous Flier's Own Story of His Life and His Transatlantic Flight, Together with His Views on the Future of Aviation* (New York: G. P. Putnam's Sons, 1927); Lindbergh's photo albums and the map of his travels are now in the Minnesota Historical Society collections, St. Paul.

4. Grace Lee Nute correspondence in Charles A. Lindbergh and Family Papers, Minnesota Historical Society collections; Nute's planned biography of the senior Lindbergh was never completed.

5. Lindbergh to William Jovanovich, December 18, 1969, quoted in the introduction to *The Wartime Journals of Charles A. Lindbergh* (New York: Harcourt Brace Jovanovich, 1970), xi.

6. *Of Flight and Life* (New York: Charles Scribner's Sons, 1948), 30, 50–51.

7. *The Spirit of St. Louis,* with an introduction by Reeve Lindbergh (Borealis Books; St. Paul: Minnesota Historical Society Press, 1993), xv, xvi (first published by Charles Scribner's Sons, New York, in 1953).

8. *Autobiography of Values* (New York: Harcourt Brace Jovanovich, 1978), 396; Lindbergh died on August 26, 1974, on the island of Maui, Hawaii, where he and his wife, the writer Anne Morrow Lindbergh, owned a cottage.

9. *Boyhood on the Upper Mississippi: A Reminiscent Letter* (St. Paul: Minnesota Historical Society, 1972) and *Lindbergh Looks Back: A Boyhood Reminiscence* (St. Paul: Minnesota Historical Society Press, 2002); the letter is now part of the Charles A. Lindbergh and Family Papers in the society's collections. In preparing the letter for publication, only the minimum necessary explanatory information has been added in the form of footnotes or enclosed by square brackets in the text. In a few places, repetition has been eliminated, and some paragraphs have been rearranged in the interest of readability, but the material has not been rewritten. Lindbergh's brief comments on the background and circumstances under which the letter was written have been set in italic type.

Lindbergh
Looks Back

I find myself having the unusual experience of a completely free day! I expected to fly to northeastern Luzon, in a light plane I have rented, for about a week's visit with some of the "primitive" Philippine tribes, but my take-off from Manila has been postponed until tomorrow morning. ⊕ *Remembering my promise to write about some of the background of Lindbergh State Park, I shall start now. I don't know when this letter will be finished, or from where it will be mailed.*

MUST START with stories told me by my mother. The land area [of some 110 acres preserved within Charles A. Lindbergh State Park] was bought by my father [in 1898], she said, because of its beauty—the river, the creek, the pines, oaks, birches, etc.—and proximity to Little Falls, where my father had his law offices.

After graduating from [the University of Michigan at] Ann Arbor with a B.S. degree, my mother decided to teach school. When she heard of an opening for a chemistry teacher in the Little Falls High School, she visualized a mining town where she would teach the miners' children and walk back and forth to school followed by a big dog carrying her books. She was also attracted by the fact that Little Falls lay across the, to her, highly romantic Mississippi River.

As I recall, my mother said she rented a room at the Antlers Hotel on the West Side of Little Falls, and that my father also was staying there. I am under the impression that my mother and father first met at the Antlers, but I am far from sure of this. Anyway, my mother said my father was considered the handsomest man in Little

THE CABIN on the banks of the Mississippi River, where Charles, Sr., and Evangeline Lindbergh lived in 1901 while their first house was being built on the Little Falls property

Falls. (She had been described as the most beautiful girl at Ann Arbor.) They soon became engaged.*

That winter [1900] an incident arose which ended my mother's teaching [in Little Falls]. Her chemistry laboratory was on the top floor of the high school in a sort of "attic room." It was not well heated. One sub-zero winter day, my mother concluded that the room was too cold for her students and proceeded to carry the apparatus she wanted to demonstrate to her chemistry class downstairs. This was against the school regulations. On the stairs she met the high school superintendent, who said she would have to take the apparatus back to the attic. She said the attic was too cold and proceeded to continue downstairs. The superintendent blocked her way. My mother's flashing Irish temper rose. She put the apparatus on the stairs in front of the superintendent, walked out of the school, and never taught there again. Previous disagreements had

---

*The elder Lindbergh had been widowed in 1898 when his first wife, Mary LaFond Lindbergh, died, leaving him with two young daughters—Lillian and Eva.

arisen between her and the superintendent, and the tension was already high.

My father and mother were married [on March 27, 1901] in Detroit, Michigan, the home of my mother's parents, Dr. and Mrs. Charles Henry Land. On their honeymoon they visited San Francisco, Yosemite Park, and the Garden of the Gods in Colorado.

After they returned [to Little Falls], my mother said she and my father first lived in a quickly constructed cabin close to the riverbank and near a huge burr oak. Its location was almost exactly east of the present house. They lived in this cabin while the first house was being built.

That portion of the level valley lying north of a line drawn between the present house and the cabin site, and limited to approximately one to two acres of land, was planted with plum and crab-apple trees, raspberry, blackberry, gooseberry, and currant bushes. In later years, these ran wild but continued to produce as long as we lived on the farm.

My father carried on a real-estate business in addition to his law practice. He pleaded cases in the yellow brick courthouse and was attorney for the Weyerhaeuser lumber company.*

For my birth [on February 4, 1902] my mother went back to Detroit. Three of her uncles (her mother's brothers) were doctors, and one of them, Dr. Edwin Lodge, presided at my birth. Six weeks thereafter my mother and I returned to the farm at Little Falls.

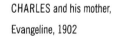

CHARLES and his mother, Evangeline, 1902

I now skip to the time when my existing memory begins, combining this with my mother's and father's stories.

The first house was furnished to a large extent with chairs, tables, settees, bookcases, etc., that my father and mother bought at Grand Rapids, Michigan. A number of these pieces are now in the

---

*The elder Charles Lindbergh was born in Sweden, probably in 1859. His father, August, had been a prominent member of the Swedish parliament before emigrating to the United States in 1860. Charles, Sr., grew up on a farm near Melrose, Stearns County, Minnesota. He attended the University of Michigan, from which he graduated in law in 1883 and soon thereafter began to practice in Little Falls.

present house in the park. I recall a well-furnished living room and a fairly large dining room containing a big dish- and silver-covered table from which my father on occasion fed me carrots. I remember a view over the Mississippi from an upstairs window, and a large downstairs front hall with a big couch on which my father often covered me with pillows. Through the house three dogs ranged—a great Dane I called Sweet Snider who used to inflict heavy blows on my head with his tail, a coach dog named Breeze, and a shepherd named Shep.

The first house was large by Little Falls standards. There were servants and much entertainment, with carriage-driving back and forth to town. I remember driving from the farm to town with my mother in a horse and carriage to play with Carl Weyerhaeuser, who was about my age. Meanwhile my mother and Mrs. Weyerhaeuser would visit. I remember evenings when many guests arrived. There would be card playing and sometimes acting.

[LUZON]

October 28, 1969

My "free day" was not as free as I expected it to be. I am now writing on the split-bamboo floor of a grass hut on the northeastern coast of Luzon, held down by clouds which cover the coastal mountain range I want to cross. Heavy rain squalls alternate with sunshine. At the moment the hut is crowded with smiling naked natives. A fire in one corner cooks rice. We breathe smoke with air, but it is not at all unpleasant. Writing will be somewhat difficult, but I have nothing else to do until the weather clears enough for me to unrope my plane and take off. That may be tomorrow, or the day after, or even later. I must wait for fairly clear weather because I don't have enough fuel left in my tanks to start and turn back again. I did that, flying alone, this morning—fifty minutes of gasoline wasted. ⊕ I should probably explain that I landed on this semiabandoned airstrip (once a logging-company airstrip) just before dark yesterday. It has been a fascinating experience. I won't mind too much if the weather stays bad. ⊕ But back to Minnesota: I write in pencil because it is so humid that the paper blots with ink.

MY NEXT VIVID RECOLLECTION is of the house burning [on August 6, 1905].* There was sudden shouting—women's voices. I was picked up quickly and taken across the road to a place behind the barn. Somehow I got to a corner of the

_____

* An account of the fire may be found in the *Little Falls Daily Transcript*, August 7, 1905, p. 3.

barn and looked around it to see a huge column of smoke billowing skyward from a corner of our house. Then I was taken back and told I mustn't look.

The house burned completely, but a great deal of furniture, silver, dishes, etc., was saved. The fire started in an upstairs corner in daytime. Men and women had considerable time to run in and out from the lower floors before it became too dangerous.

When I stood on the edge of the basement pit with my mother, it was filled with ash and twisted metal (bed frames, etc.). Only the chimney was left standing above the cellar's stone walls, and on its fireplace shelf, a Mexican idol made of red clay. Several stonelike lumps at my feet had been windowpanes.

We took rooms at the Buckman Hotel in Little Falls. For me it was a dreary place. I spent much of my time hanging over a window sill and looking down on the street below—on men, women, and children passing back and forth along the board sidewalk; on horses (carriages and wagons behind them) hitched to rails and posts; on the rutted, unpaved road; on the livery stable fronting the other side.

There were special days when my mother would rent a horse and carriage from the livery, and we would cross the river and drive [a mile and a half] southward for a picnic lunch on our farm. The road was mostly sand and ran almost exactly where the present paved road lies—often within sight of the river, over small pastures, or between scattered trees. We would pass carriages and wagons and occasionally an automobile at which our horse would shy.

Carl Bolander designed and supervised the building of the present house [in 1906]. A mason named Chilson did the stonework. He lived in a small, tar-paper-covered house a few hundred feet beyond the southern boundary of our farm, between the road and the river. I watched the house construction and climbed over the scaffolding. One of the carpenters made for me a small ladder between four and five feet high. With it I played being a fireman and explained to my sisters, Lillian and Eva, how I would put the fire out if one started in our house again.

My father was running for the national Congress about this time from the then Sixth District. I remember a good deal of talk about the campaign and the chance of my father winning. The only part I remember taking in the campaign consisted of one church attendance. (I have described this in *The Spirit of St. Louis*.) The next winter [1907] we joined my father in Washington.*

Our new house, much smaller than the first, was built on the same stone foundation. It was painted light gray with white trim on door frames, corner boards, etc. The same flower beds remained in front of the new house, planted largely with iris—probably my mother's favorite flower. There were two of these beds, oval and outlined by roundish stones. I now estimate each bed to have been about fifteen feet in length. Nasturtium is the only other flower I remember in them, but there were a number of varieties. My mother loved flowers and had made a number of very good water colors of her iris. She also liked tiger lilies. It seems to me she had some of these planted in the ovals. And now I remember there were purple violets.

My mother had ordered lilac and honeysuckle bushes planted along the road in front of the house. These ran from a few rods south of the round entrance drive to a point near the ice-house gate. There were lilacs, purple and white, on each side of the house entrance gate. Honeysuckle bushes, both pink and white, had been planted farther northward.

About halfway between the house entrance gate and the icehouse gate was the footpath gate. The depression for the footpath is still plainly visible, so this gate can be exactly located. Inside the fence and on each side of the gate were pink honeysuckle bushes. Outside the gate and a few feet to the left on top of a white cedar fence post

THE TWO Charles A. Lindberghs, father and son, about 1910

---

*Shortly after Lindbergh's election to Congress in 1907, his relationship with his wife underwent an estrangement that resulted in their maintaining separate living quarters until his death in 1924. He remained in touch with his wife, however, often visiting the home and corresponding with her almost until the end of his life. His association with his son was a close, mutually affectionate one, and he spent as much time with Charles as possible. Evangeline Lindbergh died in 1954 at her home in Detroit.

our galvanized iron mailbox (R.F.D. No. 3) was located. Mail was delivered once each weekday—at first by horse and carriage, later by car. At that time first-class postage was two cents an ounce.

The entire farm was fenced with barbed wire above sheep (net) wire stapled to white cedar posts, except the area in front of our house, where higher sheep wire (roughly 4½ feet) was used with no barbed wire above it. If my memory is right, my father said the white cedar posts cost fifteen cents each. They were round, not split. Each side of the road that ran straight the length of the farm was so fenced. The road itself was rather sandy and followed closely the eastern fence line. Hazel brush grew thick on the roadside of most of the western fence line.

The fences around our house on the north, west, and south lay almost exactly where they are today. The north and south fences ran from the road fence (at their west ends) to a fence which ran about parallel to the riverbank and about a rod and a half inland from the river. This arrangement left a passage along the riverbank and completely fenced in the house, icehouse, gardens, and orchard. A hayrack-size gate was in the fence along the riverbank, close to the site where the cabin was located. This gate was made of wood and net wire.

The house water system—a gravity system—at that time was based on a boarded-in, galvanized iron tank in the hayloft of the barn. A pipe ran underground from the barn to the house. A well had been drilled 60 feet deep, if my memory is correct, before the barn was built, so the pump was in the barn. Water for the barn loft tank was pumped by a one-cylinder gasoline engine. (The same engine that is now in the basement of the house.)

Weather, flying, and activities in the Agta village have held up the writing of these notes. At the moment, I am in a small airstrip-edge cottage in northern Luzon—a great contrast to the Agta lean-to where I slept on the sand last night with a nine-year-old boy and a dog.

AN UPRIGHT PIANO was one of the items saved at the time the first house burned. This was placed in the living room of the second house. My mother played it and sang to me when I was still quite small. I recall the titles of two of the songs: "A Spanish Cavalier" and "As We Go Marching Through Georgia."

During the first several summers we lived in the new house (often called "Camp"), my mother had the help of a general maid, Esther Carlson, the sister of Nettie Carlson who had been my nurse in the old house. Thereafter my mother did all of the housework herself.

In the usual good weather of a Minnesota summer, I spent most of my time outdoors—at first nearby the house and in later years all over our farm and in the wild "Williams Woods" northwest of our fence lines. I then often walked to neighbors' houses to play with their children—mostly to the Thompsons and the Johnsons where there were boys of about my age, Bill Thompson and Alex Johnson. The Thompson house was about a half mile north and west. The Johnson house was the second northward between our

CHARLES playing in a Minnesota lake, 1908

farm and town. We played the ordinary children's games like hide-and-seek and tag, but we boys were more likely to go swimming in the river or [Pike] creek—naked, of course.

My father taught me to love swimming in the river and creek. At first, doing the breast stroke, he carried me on his back. Then he encouraged me to wade out from the bank and swim back. In Pike Creek we swam in the deepest pool in a bend next to a sand bank. It was a bit shallow for my father but an excellent depth for me, and it was wonderful to lie in the sun on the sand between swims.

Our swimming place in the Mississippi was roughly two hundred yards to the north of our house. There a small gap passed through the mound line next to the river, and beyond the gap a flattop, granite boulder made an excellent seat when one was not in swimming. (This boulder is now covered by the dam-formed lake.) To get to our swimming place, we walked along a footpath that started just north of the house—first steep down the hillside, then flat through the valley to the riverbank, and thereafter northward. After passing the clearing where the crab-apple trees, plum trees, and berry bushes had been planted, the path entered a thick woods shaded by high branches.

The day came when, with my father, I waded out beyond my depth in the river and found myself swimming, scared, surprised, and delighted, toward the shore. I can still see the smile of proud amusement on my father's face as he stood in the water nearby. Within three or four years, I was swimming across the creek in flood and down the river's rapids. From spring to fall there was a tremendous change in the flow of the creek and the river. In August the flow of water would sometimes stop entirely in the creek, and I could wade all the way across the river.

In summer, and later in winter, I would sleep on the screened porch overlooking the river. There I was in close contact with sun, wind, rain, and stars. My bed, a wide, folding-cot affair, was in the northwest corner. On stormy nights rain blown in through the screen would mist it. Some of the valley's treetops rose slightly above its level.

At times in the summer violent thunderstorms occurred. My mother was terrified of them. When I was still quite young, she used to take me from the porch bed when she heard a storm coming at night and put me on a cot she pushed to the center of the dining room floor. Lightning struck trees on our farm a number of times —usually one of the tall pines—splitting a path through bark from tip to roots, sometimes shattering the tree to pieces. It seems to me that seldom a summer passed when at least one pine was not struck.

ARMY AND NAVY CLUB

Manila, November 5, 1969

O N RAINY DAYS I would spend a good deal of time playing in the upstairs rooms and in the basement. For a number of years after the house was built the upstairs rooms were left unfinished with no doors and rough pine floors. I had the entire floor practically for myself. As a result my toys, stone collection, and other articles of interest were well scattered about. I recall two items in particular: the rusted barrel of my father's rifle which had been retrieved from the ashes of the first-house fire, and the shell from a snapping turtle on which my father had carved his name. My father told me that after he carved his name on the turtle he had let it go and that it was found again years later. (When you and I were in the house this fall, I saw the shell in the same upstairs room where I kept it years ago.) For me, one of the attractions of the upper floor lay in the tunnels formed by the eaves. I could crawl through them and hide in them my more secret and precious possessions.

The basement had great attractions, too, especially when days were hot, for it was always cool. When the construction of the new house had been completed, leftover yellow bricks and planks were piled in the basement. I used them to build houses there, laying some of the longer planks (2 by 6 inches) across basement corners and on top ledges of foundation walls for crawlways.

In early years I also had interesting activities on nearby grounds outside the house. One of my favorite occupations consisted of walking with a pair of stilts I had made. They were high enough so

I could step onto them from our kitchen porch, and the sod around our house was usually solid enough to stilt-walk on. With Bill Thompson and Alex Johnson I dug a cave around an old stump beside the footpath to the mailbox. This started as a circular trench. Later we covered all but the entrance with boards and heaped the dugout earth on top of them.

I fastened a plank seat about ten feet above the ground in the Y of a linden tree just south of the icehouse and nailed steps to the tree trunk so I could easily climb up to it. (This tree is no longer standing.) I had another climbing tree, a big red oak, roughly twenty yards west by north of our house. The lower branches were above my reach, so I made a hole in the trunk for a railroad spike large enough so I could pull the spike out when my tree was not in use—like locking the door to our house. Here I loved to hold on to the high branches in a wind, with the trunk swaying and the leaves fluttering and white clouds drifting past overhead. (This tree, too, is no longer standing.)

Near the foot of this red oak, I built a house by nailing boards on two big sawhorses which had been left behind after the construction of our second house. This house had a special feature. After building it, I had proudly invited my father inside. Upon entering, stooped down, he had remarked that the house was not big enough for him to lie down in, and that therefore he could not very well spend the night in it (my invitation). After considerable study of the problem, I sawed out a small door for his feet at a bottom corner of one end. A hinged square of wood permitted me to close this door when it was not in use. Still, we never spent an entire night in my playhouse.

In early nighttime I would often lie on the bed with my father while he told me stories. So far as I can now remember, they were invariably about his boyhood on the old homestead near Melrose [in adjacent Stearns County]—about his hunting, fishing, and schooling; about the Chippewa Indians who camped and passed nearby; about the dangerous Sioux; about the squeaking wheels of Red River oxcarts, the coming of the railroad, and the farm and household chores.

As a boy it had been my father's job to keep the family supplied with meat—ducks, partridge, deer, prairie chicken, fish. His younger brother, Frank, was assigned such household chores as splitting wood and carrying water. Juno and Linda [his sisters] were, of course, well occupied with kitchen, garden, sewing, and washing.

Some years later when we had an automobile, my father and I drove several times to Melrose to visit the old homestead. We would drive close to the grass-grown hollow in the ground that marked the old house location, walk over the grounds, along the Sauk River banks, and over to the ruts left by the Red River oxcarts, still clearly visible but grass covered.

Like my father I grew up with guns, but I had many more of them than he, and all of mine were breech-loading. My Grandfather Land gave me at the age of six a Stevens single-shot 22-caliber rifle. My father felt I was a little young to have a real gun, but the next summer he gave me a Savage 22-caliber repeating rifle. A year or two later he gave me a Winchester automatic 12-gauge shotgun. It was so heavy that I had difficulty holding it to my shoulder, and the kick from a shot was terrific. Before this my great-uncle, Edwin

AUGUST AND LOUISA Lindbergh's farm home near Melrose, Minnesota, where their son Charles A. Lindbergh, Sr., grew up. This frame house replaced the log home built soon after the family emigrated from Sweden.

The AUGUST AND LOUISA Lindbergh family about 1873 (clockwise from left): August, Linda, Charles, Louisa holding Frank, and Juno

CHARLES at the age of six or seven with his dog and the results of a successful hunting trip

Lodge, had given me a 10-gauge saluting cannon with blank shells from his yacht. Soon afterward my uncle, Charles H. Land, Jr., gave me a single-shot 22-caliber pistol. I also had charge of a 38-caliber Smith & Wesson revolver (hammerless) that my father had kept in his house for many years. (All of these guns are now in the possession of the Minnesota Historical Society, as well as my father's double-barreled Parker 12-gauge shotgun.) I spent a great deal of time cleaning and oiling my guns and practicing target shooting.

Almost every summer, my mother and I were alarmed by shots fired from across the river. My father never happened to be on the farm when one of these incidents took place. The first shooting incident I recall was a bullet whining past our heads as my mother and I were standing on the north side of our house. We immediately went inside. The shooting was obviously to scare and not to kill—almost certainly done for amusement—although a man walking along the road to the north of our farm was hit in the leg by a bullet.

The most serious of the shooting incidents occurred when I was poling a raft off the riverbank. (I had made a raft by nailing boards onto a half dozen white cedar posts.) Bullets began splashing within five or six feet of the raft, and I heard cracks from a rifle across the river. I poled the raft to shore as quickly as I could, beached it, and climbed up over the bank and out of sight. As I recall, Bill Thompson was with me at the time, although I don't think he was on the raft, and it seems to me this was the time he and I returned the fire. Anyway, the shooting incidents had caused me to build a small earthworks on the riverbank—a shovel-scooped trench with an oblong mound of earth in front of it. Grass had grown in the trench and on the mound before I actually used them.

After the shots from the east riverbank, Bill and I raced across the valley and up the hill to our house. I grabbed my 22-caliber rifle and gave him the 10-gauge cannon. We returned to the valley and crawled (out of sight of the east bank) to our earthworks. Pushing through the grass, we saw several men and boys in a clearing across the river from us. (As I now recall there were one man—probably a young man—and four or five not fully grown boys.) The man was carrying a rifle and all were singing "Shoot the old Nigger up in the tree."

According to previous agreement, Bill took command of the cannon and I pushed my rifle through the grass, aiming far enough away from the group across the river so there would be no danger of hitting anyone and close enough so they would hear the bullet sing. I counted to three and on "three" we both fired. Of course the cannon made a tremendous noise, and the zing of the bullet was effective. The group scattered into bushes and trees, and there was no more firing that year.

On our farm I saw plenty of gophers, a few red squirrels, woodchucks, and chipmunks. A tame chipmunk lived in a rock pile a few feet northwest of our kitchen door. Sometimes I could get it to eat from my hand. I called it "Shorttail" as a result of its narrow escape from one of my dogs.

CHARLES with his tame chipmunk, Shorttail, about 1914

We had many songbirds around the house and crows were frequently heard cawing. Hawks often circled overhead. The long line of honeysuckle bushes along the road held dozens of small birds' nests. At night a few owls hooted.

The river life I saw consisted of crayfish, minnows, and snapping, mud, and soft-shelled turtles. Fishing was poor—mostly suckers. There were butterflies, dragonflies, quite a few mosquitoes, and lots of spiders.

On the farm I almost always wore blue overalls, with or without a shirt depending on mosquitoes and weather. My mother usually wore simple cotton dresses. My father always dressed in business clothes—an old pair of pants tucked inside high leather boots when we went tramping or hunting.

Aside from shooting a few crows, we did no hunting on the farm. There were no game animals or birds to hunt. Occasionally I saw ducks flying overhead, but they never landed nearby. The plentiful game of my father's boyhood had largely vanished from that part of Minnesota. In a single generation the wilderness had been replaced by farms.

Our hunting was always at some distance from the farm. At first my father took me with him in a horse-drawn carriage. Later we drove in his 1912 Ford car. There was one exception: sometimes we hunted on a farm my father owned about a mile farther down the river called the "Green Farm."* It had an old abandoned frame house surrounded by a long field of not very many acres. Most of the Green Farm was wooded, and in the woods were a few partridge. Hunting was poor. We went hunting more often on the "Estes Farm." (I cannot now locate it.) It was thickly wooded, and the woods contained quite a few partridge. There were also prairie chickens in nearby fields. Since much wild land was unfenced in those days, we would often just park our car at the roadside and hunt in the nearby woods or on the shores of a lake.

My father always carried his double-barreled 12-gauge Parker shotgun. At first I carried my Stevens and later, when I was old enough to lift it to my shoulder effectively, my Winchester 12-gauge shotgun. My father was always a better shot than I with a shotgun. Eventually I was probably able to outshoot him with a rifle, possibly because he didn't shoot a rifle very much in his later years.

FATHER AND SON on a hunting expedition about 1911. Charles, Sr., appears to be carrying his Parker shotgun.

My father never shot at birds unless they were flying. At first, when I was using a 22-caliber rifle, I was allowed to shoot at partridges on branches and ducks on water. Later, when I hunted with a shotgun, I considered such a "pot shot" beneath my dignity.

Hunting ducks, my first shot was probably my best. When I was about seven years old and hunting with my 22-caliber rifle, my father and I had crept up on some ducks near a lake shore. He let me have the first shot. I aimed at one of the ducks at a distance of more than fifty feet and hit it in the head. I don't know whether my father or I was more surprised. He brought down a second duck on the wing and our hunting dog retrieved both ducks from the water.

I was seldom without a dog while living on the farm. Tody, the first to share the new house with me, was a smallish, good-humored,

---

*The Green Farm, owned by the elder Lindbergh, was located in Morrison County, Pike Creek Township 129, range 30, section 36, SE 1/4.

CHARLES with Dingo, one of his companions on the farm. Dingo died in the fall of 1915, and Charles bought Wahgoosh the following summer.

somewhat dachshund-stretched mongrel. He was followed by Spot, a short-haired white and brown hunting dog. Spot was followed by Hunter, a mostly white, but a little brown, long-haired, overly affectionate, fairly large dog. Next came Dingo, a white-chested, red, short-haired dog who arrived at our kitchen door looking for food. We adopted him. Several years later some unknown person shot him. Last was Wahgoosh, a short-haired black and white fox terrier, named for what I was told was the Chippewa Indian word for fox. He was also shot eventually; by whom I never knew.

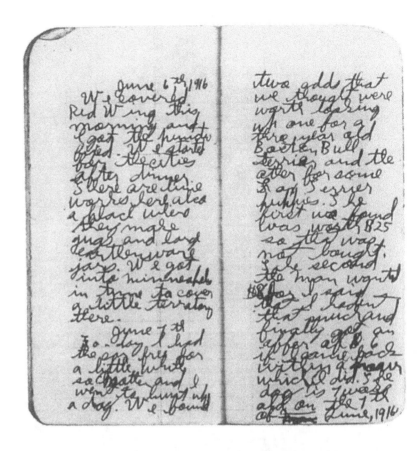

After the first house burned and until America's entry into World War I [in 1917], my mother and I spent only summers on the farm. With two exceptions, we spent our winters in Washington to be near my father while he was carrying on his duties in Congress. The first exception was our winter in Minneapolis [1908–09]. The second was the winter of 1916–17, which we spent in California.

In September my mother and I would board the train at Little Falls, change trains at Chicago, and get off at Detroit for a two-week visit at my grandparents' house. In spring we would make the return trip, again stopping for two weeks at Detroit.

Although my father kept an office in Little Falls [after 1907], he was in it only a small portion of the year. The rest of the time he was in Minneapolis, in Washington, or traveling. In my earliest memory, his office was located on the West Side of Little Falls on the ground floor and east side of the building which was later occupied by Martin Engstrom. (This side of the building became Engstrom's soft drink parlor; the other side became his hardware store.) My father shared his office with Carl Bolander, who had designed and supervised the construction of our second house. Bolander assisted my father with his real-estate business, and he was essential in this respect because of my father's extended absences.

Each side of the building had a big plate-glass window front. A big desk, usually occupied by Bolander, had been placed just inside the window of my father's office. I remember it as usually stacked with papers. In the back reaches of the office were stacks of books, boxes containing campaign literature, and, usually, two bicycles—my father's and Bolander's.

My father usually rode this bicycle between his office and the farm in those days. He would turn in on the icehouse road, dismount, and start whistling the call of the whippoorwill. This was my signal to start running with my dog up the icehouse road [to meet him]. Father and I would go for a swim, tramp over the farm, and return to the house for a lunch cooked by my mother.

CHARLES LINDBERGH, SR., represented the Minnesota's sixth congressional district from 1907 to 1917. Here young Charles is standing near his father at the opening of the 60th Congress in 1907.

23

Sometimes we would go down to the river and walk out on log jams. These jams were often quite big. As I recall, it was twice each summer that the bateaux and wanigans came through to clear them. Then the "river pigs" would give exhibitions of logrolling and break up the seemingly unbreakable jams.

Log-driving time always brought at least one free meal to the children of the farms on the riverbank. Lumber companies were eager to keep on good terms with the farmers who owned the land over which the log drivers often walked, and one way to do this lay in extending mealtime hospitality. My father first took me to a river-pig meal. Thereafter I arrived alone or with the neighbor boys. The meals were heavy, good, and unlimited in quantity—big chunks of meat, potatoes, and carrots, dippered out onto tin plates, if my memory is correct. You could go back for more as often as you wished. And after lunch, you had the privilege of watching as long as you wished the expert plying of peavey and pike pole.

Before my father bought his first automobile in 1912, transportation between our farm and town was somewhat of a problem. On getting off the train at the Little Falls station in June, my mother would order meat at Wilczek's market and groceries at Ferguson's grocery store, and then usually arrange for the Ferguson one-horse delivery cart to pick up our trunks and suitcases at the station and deliver them to our house.

During the summer we would get a delivery from the Ferguson store about once a week. In between I would often walk or bicycle to town for fresh meat and miscellaneous items. As I grew older I did a good deal more bicycling than walking. At first I rode a small bicycle that had been given to me in Detroit by my grandfather. Later I found that my father's bicycle was much easier to pedal—even though I had to ride it "underbar" because my legs wouldn't reach the pedals when I sat on the seat.

With week-apart food deliveries from town, an icebox was quite important to us. In addition to meat and vegetables, the icebox let us keep fresh milk which we got from the tenant who ran our farm. It was my job to fill the box with ice, and in early years this was a formidable task because of the weight of the ice. (I felt it beneath my dignity to split the cakes in half.)

The icehouse was filled with big ice cakes, cut from the Mississippi in winter from an area above the Little Falls dam. Of course these cakes were always surrounded by sawdust to keep them from melting during hot summer months. I would shovel the sawdust off a cake, split it carefully into smaller chunks of a size that would just fit into our icebox, and then with a pair of tongs drag one of the chunks up on top of the sawdust. Since it was too heavy for me to lift up out of the icehouse onto the ground, I had constructed a slide from 2-by-6-inch planks. With a rope attached to the tongs, it was not difficult for me to pull the ice chunks up the slide. Then I would tip my express cart over on its side, push the ice chunk up against it, and tip the cart upright again. I would pull the cart to a stake in the ground well in front of the kitchen steps, to which I had fastened one end of a heavy wire. The other end of the wire I had attached to a ring screw embedded in the house wall above the kitchen porch. I would hook the ice tongs to a pulley that ran over this wire and then haul the pulley, with tongs and ice, up on top of the porch. From there it was easy to slide the ice chunk over floors and into the pantry where we kept the icebox against the north wall. There I had another slide, also made of planks, to get the ice into its compartment.

Not long after the first house burned, my father stopped running the farm himself and turned the operation over to a tenant.* The first of these was a milk farmer by the name of Stevens. With the help of his two sons, Ernest and Chester, he ran the farm and also a milk route. I recall that Stevens was followed by a tenant named Gill, who had several children, two of them close to my age, with whom I played in the stables and hayloft. At the time I took over the running of the farm, soon after the United States entered World War I, the tenant was named Gertz. A man in his mid-thirties, he had a background of tenant farming along with somewhat radical political views. He ran our farm "on shares."

As far back as I can remember after the new house was built, we had a vegetable garden to the south of it and close to the road. Here the tenant would plant some vegetables before my mother and I arrived in June, and we would plant quicker growing seeds, such as

---

*The tenant's house was located across the road beyond the barn.

Dear Father,
I am glad that you got a man for the place. I want to ask you several questions.
1 Has he a wife?
2 Has he any children?
3 What is his name?
4 Can I keep the auto in the barn?
5 What ... does Stevens leave?
6 Will you stay in Minn till I get there?
7 Can I have the first copy of your book?
8 Have you heard anything about Dingy?
9 When will I get my duck boat?
10 When will I get my duck car?
11 When will I get my tool kit?
12 ... are you going to get me something?
13 are you going to get me any chickens?
14 are you going to get many ducks?
15 Will you have my automobile ready at the office when I get there

I expect to get there about the first of June

Charles

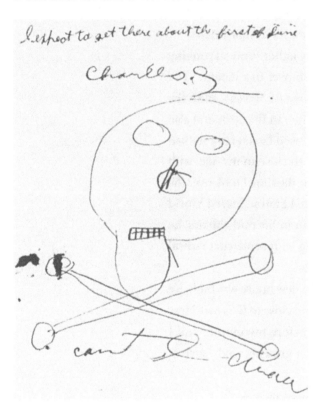

IN MAY 1913, Charles wrote this letter from Detroit to his father with fifteen questions about the new hired man for the farm and other matters vital to an eleven-year-old boy.

lettuce and radish, after our arrival. My mother and I took care of the garden, hoeing, raking, and weeding. It furnished us with potatoes, carrots, beets, cabbages, tomatoes, ground cherries, and corn (Golden Bantam and Minnesota white). My mother also planted flowers in the garden at one edge. When the tomatoes were ripe, my father loved to pull them off the vines and eat them with a little salt. I ate them, too, but I liked best of all the sweet corn my mother cooked.

She cooked on a wood stove, a Majestic. We used wood sticks and slabs from the sawmill [in Little Falls] because they were easy to get and cheap. A team of sawmill horses would bring a load at a time in a specially constructed box wagon and dump it a few yards north of our kitchen door. Most of the sticks were just the right size for our stove. I split the slabs with an ax. We had a big wood box in the kitchen between the sink and the outside door. I kept it full of stovewood, so we would always have a dry supply.

My mother's dishes were simple and wonderfully good. She fried, boiled, baked, and roasted. We usually had meat three times a day, along with vegetables, salads, and fruits. For dessert we had pies (apple, peach, berry, pumpkin, gooseberry), puddings (bread, tapioca, plum), cakes (angel, chocolate), and cookies of various types. My mother often made a Swedish butter cookie—very rich, yellow, and in the form of an O. She got the recipe from Alex Johnson's mother. This was my favorite cookie. We made ice cream on occasion in a churn packed with cracked ice and salt. My mother usually baked our bread herself—white, rye, white salt-rising, and potato bread. For breakfast she would often bake biscuits. It was seldom that we were without home-made jam and cottage cheese, which she made from sour milk.

My mother's frying pans were black iron. She had a heavy aluminum tea-kettle, but most of her pots were enamel. Sometimes we ate on the porch but more often in the kitchen on an oblong, woodtopped table. We used ordinary kitchen plates and silver, although my mother had more elaborate dishes that had been saved from the first-house fire. Among these were Chinese plates—some decorated with small Chinese figures—which she and my father had bought in San Francisco during their honeymoon. (The Minnesota Historical Society now has these plates.)

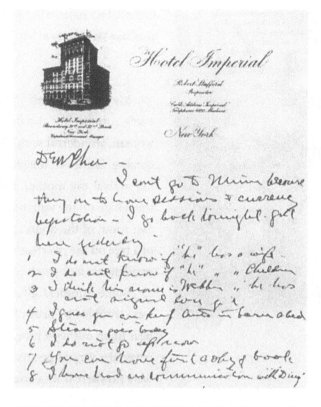

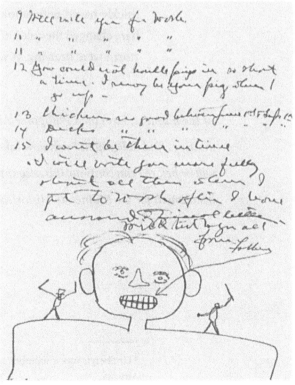

27

GRANDMOTHER Evangeline Land on the screened porch, with Dingo on her lap, in a photograph taken about 1914, probably by Charles

My Grandmother [Evangeline Lodge] Land came to visit us every summer for the month of August. She was a kindly, quiet woman, wonderful with children. I always looked forward to her coming. She loved the smell of pine, so a day or two in advance of her arrival my mother and I would get pine boughs and fasten them high on the walls of her room. She always stayed in the northeast room of the house. My grandmother loved to sit in the shade of a tree on the riverbank, and she and my mother often visited the maidenhair fern patch in the valley close to the foot of the hill.

Some summers, after a stretch of hot weather with no rain, we were troubled by brush fires. My mother and I always managed to beat them out with pine boughs before they did much damage or covered a very large area. The pine trees on and around our farm were nowhere thick enough to support a forest fire, but great forest fires occurred farther north in the state. I remember seeing the sky thickly hazed with smoke from a northern forest fire. The smoke haze changed the color of the clouds, as though a strange and titanic storm were brewing. It was a rather terrifying sight.

At the moment, I am on a Philippine Airlines jet nearing Hong Kong. Since airline meetings and obligations* will now take over for a time, I do not know how long it will be before I can continue this account. I send these forty-one pages to you as a first installment for the Minnesota Historical Society's files on the park.

---

*Lindbergh was a member of the board of directors of Pan American World Airways.

This installment goes to you from Frankfurt. You should have already received
envelopes 1 and 2 mailed in Hong Kong.

"MARIA" impacted on our farm life in 1912. Pronounced as is the farm crop, rye, Maria was a Ford Model T tourabout with Ford's standard foot-pedal gearshift, four-cylinder engine, smooth-faced clincher-rim tires, carbide headlights, hand crank, squeeze rubber-bulb horn, folding waterproof cloth top, and quick fasten-on side curtains for rainy days. My father bought the car partly for campaigning and partly for farm transportation. My mother named it.

It is difficult now to realize the full impact that Maria had. Automobiles in 1912 were still something at which to marvel. Before Maria arrived they seemed almost as separate from our everyday lives as a show upon a stage. The fact that *my* father had bought an automobile was startling and amazing. It took my mother and me a long time to get accustomed to this new member of our family. Maria remained an unassimilated stranger for at least a year or two—many months after my father, my mother, and I had learned to drive it.

My father had not given us much warning of his purchase, as though he had wanted it to be a major surprise. It seemed that Maria just turned up suddenly in the driveway outside our door, black and shining with Clifton Roberts at the steering wheel and my father

GRANDMOTHER Land in the front seat of Maria, the Lindberghs' Ford Model T, perhaps with Charles at the steering wheel, probably about 1914

learning to drive. (Clifton Roberts was the brother of Loren Roberts, my sister Lillian's husband.) Of course, I was given a ride right away.

In 1912 learning to drive an automobile was a formidable and extraordinary experience—more a stunt than a necessity. A car didn't replace a horse; it simply let you go a little faster than a horse could go when everything was right—when roads were good in summertime and when you could get the engine started. To pull through deep ruts or during winter months, of course, you would still use a horse.

In our family my father learned to drive first. He was not much interested in mechanics and handling a car did not come easily to him. He let me ride in the back seat while he was learning. I remember particularly one occasion. He was at the wheel with Cliff Roberts sitting beside him. We started from in front of our house, rounded the driveway, turned south on the road, and chugged along satisfactorily for several hundred yards. Then my father decided to practice turning Maria around.

After swinging quite properly toward the west, he backed up with excellent technique, but intending to move forward again, he hit the wrong pedal with his foot and pushed hard into reverse. Fortunately, we hit the net wire fence between two of its white cedar posts. You could hear some squeaking of metal and several staples flew out, but no real damage was done; there were hardly any marks on the paint.

My mother didn't take as many driving lessons as my father. She was rather afraid of Maria. But the opportunity of getting back and forth to town with a vehicle that could carry meat, groceries, and other items overcame her resistance to driving it. At least she could go slowly and stop whenever she wanted.

During our first several trips between the farm and Little Falls, my mother never let the engine get out of low gear except to stop the car. This was a great strain on her leg muscles, because you had to push hard on the clutch pedal to keep a Model T in low gear.

Sometimes her leg gave out, and we just stopped. Then she kept the engine running, because if it stopped we might not be able to start it again. Of course we would arrive in town with the radiator boiling, but then we could switch off the engine and let it cool. If we couldn't start it, there would be men around to help us.

My mother was lightly built and not very strong. I did most of the engine starting. At the age of ten, I could easily lift the crank upward against the compression, but I didn't have enough weight to push it down on the other side in order to keep the engine turning. This made starting much more difficult. Sometimes my mother and I would work for an hour or more to get Maria going, especially in cold September weather. One had to be cautious starting those Model Ts. Their engines often kicked back, and if you had your thumb around the crank you were likely to get it broken. For this reason I always kept my thumb on the same side [of the crank] as my fingers.

Automobiles were seldom driven on Morrison County country roads in winter during the 1912 period, and they were never driven when there was much snow. They were primarily warm weather vehicles. One winter driving problem lay in the fact that the spread of sled runners was considerably less than that of automobile wheels, so even when sleds had packed down the snow, autos couldn't follow in their tracks. It was several years later that state laws required wide-bunk sleds—against considerable opposition by farmers.*

The attitude toward automobiles in the general 1912 period is exemplified by a farmer who gave me a ride to town on his lumber wagon. I had been walking northward along the road when his team of horses caught up to me. He called to me to climb on board. I sat on the wagon seat with him. Soon afterward an automobile approached and the horses began shying. The car stopped—a usual procedure for those days. The farmer asked me to hold the reins, jumped off the wagon, took the bridle of a horse in each hand,

———

*A law requiring that sled runners measure at least four feet, six inches, from center to center was passed by the Minnesota legislature on April 5, 1919, and became effective in 1921. *Minnesota Laws,* 1919, p. 192.

swung the team to the side of the road, and buried the horses' heads in hazel bushes. The automobile ground by and the farmer led the horses back to the road and climbed onto the wagon. I handed him the reins. We jolted on silently for several minutes. Then he turned to me and said, "If they ever get them things so you can drive 'em with reins, I guess there'll be quite a lot of 'em."

I learned to drive in 1913 at the age of eleven. I had become fascinated by automobiles in general and by Maria in particular. By 1914 I was driving our car most of the time when I was in it. My mother seldom drove it thereafter. When my father drove, I usually rode on the running board, hanging on to the struts which supported the car's folding top. (The running board on a Ford in those days was wide, giving plenty of room to stand on.) I could pick leaves off branches as we passed, and sometimes when the going was slow, scoop up a stone from the road. I liked the wind on my face and through my hair. It was much more fun than riding inside.

In the summer of 1913 after I learned to drive, my mother and I often made daylong trips with Maria to Brainerd, St. Cloud, Swanville, Royalton, Pierz, Fort Ripley—to all of the nearby towns and villages. Maria gave us a freedom of travel we had never dreamed of before. Almost always we carried a picnic lunch, and when possible we found a lake shore on which to eat it. Then we would hunt for carnelians on the beach. Several times we found a carnelian arrowhead. There were lots of lake shores and very few fences in those days. Many of the smaller lakes had no buildings whatever around them.

EVANGELINE Lindbergh with Dingo on the shore of Mille Lacs Lake, Minnesota, about 1914

None of the country roads were paved, and only a few of the more important highways had even a macadam surface. It was easy to get stuck in sand or ruts with an automobile, especially on the farm and woods roads leading to a lake shore. We often got stuck with Maria, although I soon became expert at judging when we could get through and when we couldn't.

When we got stuck, I would get the screw jack from its place under the seat, and my mother and I would start collecting stones, sticks, and branches. I

would dig out a place for a stone under the stuck wheel's axle, use it as a footing for the jack, and raise the wheel high enough to get sticks and brush beneath it. Then we would lay down sticks and brush ahead of the wheels to reach a more solid area of road. Since our tires were narrow and had no tread, at times we worked long and hard before reaching solid road again.

CHARLES LINDBERGH, SR., campaigning for Congress at Zippel in northern Minnesota in 1914. Charles, who was then twelve, drove his father about the state during this campaign.

There were trips on which my mother and I went together; others on which we took Bill Thompson or Alex Johnson with us. Neighbor children loved to ride in our car—it was probably as much of a thrill for a child as it is for a present-day boy or girl to ride in a roller coaster.

From 1913 on I drove my father on a number of his campaign trips through the Sixth District. We encountered all kinds of road conditions and often got stuck. One rainy evening in the country, he, two other men, and I got on a road that was so bad, and we got stuck so often, that we gave up trying to reach the town for which we were headed and spent the night on the parlor floor of a road-side farm house. The farmer could give us only two blankets, but we kept the stove burning enough to stay warm in spite of our half-soaked clothes.

On campaign trips my father and I often spent our nights in small-town hotels. The cost was usually one dollar a day. Meals cost between twenty-five and fifty cents. We stayed in simple rooms; in memory I see a white-painted iron bed, a light hanging down from the center of the ceiling, a wooden dresser, and two portable white crockery washbasins with pitchers inside filled with water.

I usually distributed campaign literature—pamphlets and extracts from the *Congressional Record*—in the halls and on the farms where my father spoke. Since there were no loudspeakers, my father's voice was always high [for volume]. His words were clear and easy to understand. I listened to his speeches but had little interest in politics or in issues my father discussed so often and seriously. While I wanted very much to have my father win, my primary interest in his campaign trips lay in the opportunity they gave me to be with him and to drive Maria.

Most of our driving was done by day, but there were also night drives over country roads. The headlights of 1912 Ford cars ran on calcium carbide. We carried with us a can of carbide lumps in order to replenish a used charge. The gas generator was on the running board, a polished brass affair, cylindrical and standing upright. The lower portion of the cylinder contained the calcium carbide lumps. The upper portion contained water. When you needed headlights, you turned on a valve that allowed water to drip on the carbide. This generated gas. When the gas reached the headlights, you hinged open their brass-rimmed glass doors and lit the burners. It was hard to get just the right adjustment on the water valve. The flow tended to be too high or too low, usually too low.

Sometimes my father drove at night; sometimes I did. One tended to get sleepy on a long drive. There were moments when I could hardly keep my eyes open. My father usually knew when this was the case and would insist on taking the wheel. Then to keep from getting sleepy himself he would often start singing. Actually it was more shouting. He would shout at the top of his voice as we drove through the night.

It was easy to get lost at night, and sometimes we did. Signposts were few and far between, and the roads were not well blazed. It was easy enough to miss a blaze mark in the daytime; it was much easier at night. The blaze marks consisted of different colors of paint. There was a blue trail, a red trail, a yellow trail, a red and blue trail, etc. The marks were mostly on fence posts and telephone poles and sometimes on rocks.

After we had driven the Ford about three years, we sold it and bought a Saxon Six [in 1916] from Farrow's garage [in Little Falls]. The Saxon had the tremendous advantage of an electric starter, but it was by no means as rugged a car. Its six-cylinder engine ran more smoothly than the Model T's four-cylinder, and you didn't feel road bumps as much as with the Ford. But with the Saxon we had a lot more engine and spring trouble, and it was considerably more expensive to run. Also it got stuck more easily on bad roads. Although it was a little faster than the Ford, roads were seldom good enough to let us use its extra speed. I remember passing a "25 mile speed limit" sign on the way to Minneapolis and wondering why anybody would want to go faster.

About the time we bought the Saxon, my father, at my suggestion, walled in the open area of the house east of the basement foundation and under the screened porch and northeast bedroom. This made an excellent, oversized garage, and in this area I serviced our Saxon Six automobile, including a motor overhaul, replacing piston rings, and grinding valves.

In addition to holding the Saxon, the garage gave me room to build a boat. It was a twelve-foot, flat-bottomed boat with straight sides, pointed at each end, and constructed of three-fourth-inch pine boards. It was not very stable, but it was light enough for me to lift out of the water and carry up the riverbank easily. It offered good cross-river transportation for my dog, Wahgoosh, and me. The river was so swift and usually so full of shallow rapids that my use of the boat was confined to two or three hundred yards up and downstream.

I also had a sixteen-foot clinker-built rowboat [constructed of overlapping boards]—the one my father and I used in coming

CHAS. A. LINDBERGH

Republican Candidate for
Re-Election As

CONGRESSMAN

SIXTH · DISTRICT · MINNESOTA

ONE OF the campaign posters used by Congressman Lindbergh

THE SAXON SIX purchased by
Charles Lindbergh, Sr., in 1916

down the Mississippi River from Lake Itasca [in 1915].* But it was too heavy for me alone to drag out of the water and up the bank as a regular procedure. The bank ran steeply up, roughly six or eight feet above the river depending on the height of water. Danger from floating logs and possible theft made me hesitate to leave my boats in the water.

In 1916 my mother and I planned a trip to California. We would drive there in the Saxon. It would be a great adventure and experience. I had never been west of Minnesota, and I could go to school in California during the winter. We left our farm in the late summer and my Uncle Charles went with us. I did all of the driving; neither my mother nor uncle had learned to drive the Saxon. We encountered a great deal of bad weather and many miles of poor roads—sometimes literally impassable, as in Missouri after a rain

---

*The two Lindberghs left Lake Itasca, the source of the Mississippi in north-central Minnesota, on June 19, 1915, and rowed, and on one occasion were towed, down the river as far as Cass Lake, where they arrived on June 24. The following fall they returned to Cass Lake and proceeded down the river to Aitkin, Minnesota.

where we had to stay at a small-town hotel until the clay road dried. Our trip to the coast took close to forty days.

I went to high school at Redondo Beach that winter. We returned to Minnesota the next summer (1917); again the trip took close to forty days. My mother and I were alone on this return trip. My uncle had gone back to Detroit by train soon after we reached California.

The year 1917 had a heavy impact on our family. The United States entered World War I. It was the last year of my father's five terms in Congress. While we were in California, my mother received word that Grandmother Land was dying from cancer. I entered Little Falls High School that fall—the senior class. At the same time, my father was laying plans to stock the farm with sheep and cattle the following spring. Food would be needed badly during the war, he said.

That was the first winter anyone had lived in our house, and considerable preparation was required. We had storm windows put on and the upstairs rooms further finished. This was done by a skillful carpenter, but I recall being shocked at the wages we paid him—fifty cents an hour! With the help of neighbor boys, paid by the hour, I had dug an open well in the basement's northwest corner. It seems to me we went down about twenty-five feet, mostly through a gray shale. We dug with pick and shovel and hoisted the earth up to the surface with rope and bucket. After digging, we curbed the well with curved concrete blocks. I installed a small gasoline engine and pump in the basement and a pressure tank—doing all the plumbing myself.

Martin Engstrom installed for us a hot-air furnace with the accompanying pipes. (This is the furnace now in the house.) To keep the house well heated, the furnace required too much wood, so we burned only enough to keep some warmth in the basement and in the rooms we used infrequently. Our additional heat came

WAHGOOSH looking out a rear window of the Saxon en route to California in 1916 in a photograph taken by Charles or his mother

WAHGOOSH on the porch of the cottage at Redondo Beach, California, where Charles and his mother lived in 1916–17

from the kitchen cookstove and the wood stove in the sewing room, the little room north of the dining room. During cold months, we lived almost entirely in the kitchen, the sewing room, and the bedroom north of the sewing room.

As usual, I found school difficult that winter, especially so because of my attraction to the farm. I got along fairly well in physics and mechanical drawing. Other subjects I found more tedious, and for me much homework seemed impossible. When I returned to the farm after school, there were always outdoor duties pressing, more essential and attractive than schoolwork. When they were finished and supper eaten, I was usually too sleepy to read many pages in my textbooks.

When there wasn't too much snow on the path, I bicycled back and forth to high school, often returning to our farm for lunch. When the snow was thick, I walked to school. Of course it was cold in winter when the thermometer dropped toward thirty below. (Once it reached forty below on our farm.) Then I would pull my fur cap down over my ears and draw my sheepskin coat collar forward of my nose. Frost would form on the front of my cap, on the edges of my collar, on nostril hairs.

I slept on the screened porch during most of the winter, no matter how cold it was. I would undress in the warm sewing room, put on an old fur-lined coat of my father's, open the window, and climb through it onto the bed. The bed was piled high with blankets and quilts. Often Wahgoosh would sleep with me. On some very cold winter nights, the stars were extraordinarily bright. I would look out at the constellations before falling asleep. At intervals a tree, stressed too much by the cold, would crack through the still night like a rifle shot.

My mother had brought my grandmother from Detroit to the farm, where the air was fresh and her room was filled with pine boughs. Grandmother died that winter [January 6, 1919].* My mother had taken care of her constantly for months, day and night toward the end. Her body was returned to Detroit for burial.

---

*Obituaries of Mrs. Land appear in the *Little Falls Daily Transcript*, January 7, 1919, p. 2, and the *Little Falls Herald*, January 10, 1919, p. 1.

In high school my marks fell so low that I doubt very much I could have passed the final examinations required for graduation. I was rescued by World War I. At a general assembly meeting in late winter, the principal announced that food was so badly needed in connection with the war that any student who wanted to work on a farm could leave school and still receive full academic credit just as though he had attended his classes and taken examinations. Farm workers would be badly needed to replace the men drafted for military service. I left classes as soon as school regulations permitted and returned only to receive my diploma [in 1918].

Before leaving school I had already started making plans for the future of the farm. I felt we should have a clear-cut program. After talking to my father and to various farmers, and after studying data in books and pamphlets, I decided to buy and breed toward Guernsey cattle, Duroc-Jersey hogs, Shropshire sheep, leghorn chickens, and Toulouse geese. I concluded that the farm should be mechanized and ordered a La Crosse three-wheeled tractor with a two-gang plow. Later I ordered and installed an Empire milking machine and took on the Empire agency for the general Little Falls area.

The tractor had big, metal-rimmed, lugged wheels and a two-cylinder engine. I used it for many kinds of farm work but primarily for plowing. With it I bought a two-gang plow, which was the only implement designed to fit the tractor. All the other implements I pulled with the tractor were designed for horses—wagon, harrow, disc, seeder, manure spreader, etc.

The tractor was often hard to start, and it was slow by present-day standards. Its operation was not very efficient—hooked onto the end of the implement tongue intended for a team of horses—especially on the turns at a field end. It was also rough riding with its iron tires and wheels, which jolted heavily against rocks in the fields and crossing Pike Creek.

Early that spring (1918), my father's carload of western heifers and sheep arrived. I helped drive them down from the railroad yard to the farm. As I recall, there were about twenty bred heifers (which might loosely have been called Shorthorns, mostly red and white) and about forty bred ewes (which might, as loosely, have been called

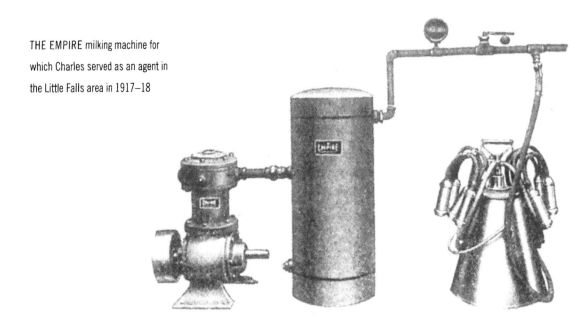

THE EMPIRE milking machine for which Charles served as an agent in the Little Falls area in 1917–18

Southdowns—white-faced). The heifers, being from western ranges, were pretty wild.

I bought a registered Guernsey bull from M. M. Williams and a registered Shropshire ram I don't now remember from whom. Later I bought from Williams a full-blooded Guernsey cow. I bought two or three incubators and also made one, and we kept them in the otherwise unused dining room. We hatched about a thousand chickens in addition to a few ducks and geese and shipped them by rail to market in Minneapolis. (A chicken house had been built northwest of our house, east of the fence row of honeysuckle bushes. I built fenced-in areas for this chicken house of net wire

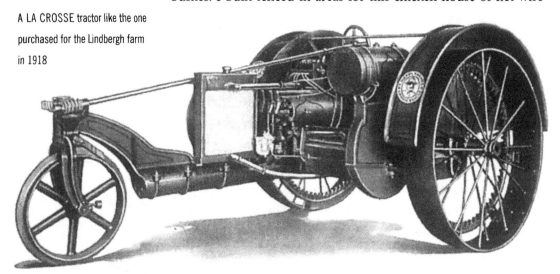

A LA CROSSE tractor like the one purchased for the Lindbergh farm in 1918

attached to galvanized iron or split white oak posts.)

About this time Daniel Thompson entered our farm life. A lanky, pipe-smoking Norwegian about seventy years of age, he had been a lumberjack in earlier years and now wanted a place to retire on his slender income. My father had known him for a number of years and offered to pay him a modest amount in return for some work on the farm. Thompson lived in the tenant's house. He helped with the sheep and cattle, with fence repairing and haying, with difficult cases of calf and lamb delivery, and with the endless tasks that arise from day to day on a farm. For me he was a tremendous asset.

Among his other abilities, Thompson was, of course, an expert axman. He could fell a tree with amazing speed, considering his age. I had to restrict his activities in this respect, because he tended to look on trees as overgrown weeds. His idea was to get rid of trees and stumps in order to get land ready for the breaking plow.

PLEASANT HOME LIZA, one of the Lindberghs' Red Polls, and her registration certificate

Thompson and I built two log houses for the Duroc-Jersey hogs, cutting trees of suitable size from the wood lot north of our western fields, barking them, notching them, and fitting them roughly to one another. Thompson did most of the axwork. After the log walls had been raised and the roofing finished, I chinked the logs with cow manure. Thereafter the log sheds were windproof and warm on hog winter standards. I hung logs around the walls inside, about six inches off the floor, to keep the sows from crushing their young against the walls.

I don't now remember which year it was that I built a suspension bridge across Pike Creek. We had needed a bridge for a long time. When the creek was low, it was easy enough to cross by jumping from stone to stone. But when the creek was high, you had either to swim or ride a horse across. I once stripped and swam across it when ice was on the water. Since our sheep scattered all over our farm, it was especially necessary to cross the creek in lambing season, when the water was usually high and cold.

When I decided to build the bridge, the only wire I had available was barbed. So I constructed it of barbed wire, split white oak fence posts, and ironwood poles. It was not difficult. On each bank of the creek I sank two fence posts deep into the ground with two or more posts sunk deeply behind them—all spaced for a bridge about three and a half feet in width. Then, strand after strand, I wound an end of barbed wire around the bases of two aligned posts, stretched the wire tightly across the creek with a block and tackle, stapled it to the bases of two corresponding posts, cut the wire long and wound the free end around the base of the most distant post. After stretching and fastening several strands of barbed wire to the bases of the posts on each side of the bridge-to-be, I hung several strands loosely above them, resting on the post tops, which were about three and a half feet above the ground. Then at intervals of about two and a half feet I wired ironwood poles between the two groups of tightly stretched lower strands, and at each ironwood pole's end position I wired the lower taut strands to the upper sagging strands. The result was a bridge of considerably more strength than was necessary to support the weight of a man crossing.

Because of the barbs Thompson and I used a special technique in crossing the bridge. We kept ironwood poles at the bridge ends, each pole about two feet longer than the width of the bridge. When we wanted to cross, we picked up one of the poles, placed it across the upper, sagging strands of barbed wire, held the pole near its center with both hands, and stepped from one bridge crossbar to the next, moving the ironwood pole forward an equal distance with each step. The barbs aided by keeping the pole from sliding along the wire strands. Later I wired boards to the ironwood crossbars. That made the walking easier, but we still used the ironwood pole.

Minnesota winters then, as now, were long and cold. Between sleeping on the porch and carrying on farm chores, I was in close touch with them. Walking to the chicken coop or barn in early morning, I could tell the approximate temperature by the bite of air in my nose and the way the snow crunched underfoot. The next sign of cold would be the thickness of ice in the barn water trough.

We let cattle and sheep out twice a day for water, but in sub-zero weather they soon returned to the barn. Then Thompson and I would distribute grain and bran and pitch down hay from the loft.

The barn was oblong in form with an inverted V-shaped, wood-shingled roof which had two cupolas for doves on top. It was painted light gray with white trim like all of our farm buildings. The barn was set broadside to the north and south. The horse stable and a long carriage room, which we had often used as a garage for Maria, were at the east end facing the road, about fifty feet away. West of these were the cow stable holding roughly sixteen cows, a pump room, saw room, and milk room which held the cream separator, milk pails, cans, and equipment. At the west end the barn was divided into two levels plus the hayloft, which ran the length of the barn. The middle level was reached by climbing up four or five wooden steps on the south side of the barn and contained a tool-room, grain bins, and extra room for storage. The lower level contained another cow stable much like the other one. Extending from the west end of the barn was a sheepshed with a low, slanting roof and doors opening on the south. With the exception of a stone foundation, the barn and shed were built of wood.

December 27, 1969

I continue this letter-account about the old farm (park) under somewhat unusual circumstances. I have been working on a manuscript* in a small room on the tenth floor of the Trade Department of Harcourt, Brace & World. Today is a holiday for the company, and only two or three members of the staff have been in their offices. The last of them—a young lady who was working with me on the manuscript—left about 17:00 [5:00 P.M.]. I stayed on for another two hours to finish going over a manuscript draft. I have done this before in these offices, sometimes working as late as 22:00 [10:00 P.M.]. ⊕ Tonight I turned out the lights at about 19:00 [7:00 P.M.], stepped into the elevator hall, and pushed the "down" button. No light and no action! Either the elevators are turned off or out of order. The door to the Trade Department quite properly locked automatically behind me, and it is the only door—aside from those of six elevators—in the hall. ⊕ I have tried shouting at the elevator doors and into the ceiling ventilator with no success, and the elevator buttons remain useless. I don't much want to spend the night here and besides tomorrow is Sunday. I might have to spend two nights before anyone arrives. I have decided to simply wait for an hour or two in the hope that the elevators will begin working again. If they don't I'll try to break the Trade Department door in. ⊕ A problem here—there's nothing available to break it in with except a large ceramic cigarette receptacle. But I've got big feet and good shoulders. ⊕ It seems a good time to continue writing the farm history. Fortunately I have the last pages with me in my brief case. I sit on the floor in a corner of the elevator hall.

---

* *The Wartime Journals of Charles A. Lindbergh* (New York: Harcourt Brace Jovanovich, 1970).

W E HAD NEITHER electricity nor a telephone on the farm. Our house was lit by kerosene lamps, the barn by kerosene lanterns. Both gave a soft and lovely light—plenty of light to read by, to milk by, to feed by—if you kept the chimneys clean. Of course it is not as convenient, but personally I prefer kerosene light to electric.

In winter I would light my lantern in the late afternoon and start out for the chicken coop and barn, usually carrying a bucket of water in one hand and a lantern and a bucket of warm bran mix for the ducks, geese, and chickens in the other. I kept sacks of grain and bran in the house pantry and mixed the bran with hot water. On the way to the chicken coop, I would pass the goose house, a small structure where we wintered only three geese—Hooligan, Fanny, and Matilda. (My mother had names for many of our animals and birds.) At the goose house I would dump half the bucket of water into a shallow tub. The geese would go for it immediately, even in thirty-below-zero weather, honking and curving their necks. Once in the water they would squat down and preen themselves until sometimes every feather would be covered with ice. They would then eat some of the warm bran I had thrown out and go back to the water again. Water for the geese was somewhat of a problem in winter because it would freeze so quickly and split the vessel that contained it. I would have to dump out whatever water was left when I returned from the chicken coop and before going on to the barn.

On cold sub-zero nights I kept a lantern burning in the chicken coop, but we had no heat whatever in the barn. The problem was to keep enough fresh air coming in without letting the milk cows get too cold. Of course all the windows would be covered thickly with frost, and the doors would be outlined in white.

After I installed a milking machine, I did the milking myself. Thompson would help with the "stripping."* It was a bit of a job to get our western, first-calf cows to accept the teat cups—a good deal

---

*Early milking machines required that the cow be milked by hand after the machine was removed to ensure that all the milk was out of the udder.

THE ABANDONED log buildings on the western forty of the Lindbergh farm, about 1921

of mooing and kicking at first—but the milking machine turned out to be a tremendous saving in time and effort.

With the feeding, milking, and separating over, I would walk back along the icehouse road to our house. I still remember clearly the heel crunch of sub-zero snow, and the occasional cracking of a tree in the distance. Back at the house, I would usually read for a time in the warm kitchen by the light of a kerosene lamp—books, the Little Falls and Minneapolis papers, magazines, farm publications. The story I remember best, although I do not now recall any of the details, related to one "Tam o' the Scoots," a magazine serial about a mythical World War I fighter pilot who soon, of course, became an ace.* I think this story had considerable effect on my decision to enlist in the army when I was old enough and to become a fighter pilot myself.

The *Minneapolis Tribune* had a section entitled something like "favorite poems of famous people." I was much impressed by the fact that the Minneapolis fire chief selected "The Cremation of Sam McGee" as his favorite poem. The *Tribune* carried the poem in full, and I memorized it as well as several other poems of Robert Service.

---

* "Tam o' the Scoots," by Edgar Wallace, ran in *Everybody's Magazine* (vols. 37–40) from November, 1917, to June, 1919. Ten of the nineteen stories were published in book form under the same title in 1919.

In winter Thompson and I did considerable woodcutting, mostly by ax. After cleaning up any dead wood available, we used the wooded area at the northwest corner of the farm as our firewood supply. Nearby were the log buildings—a house and two barns—abandoned as far back as my memory can go on land my father bought originally. They were built of adzed logs and had peaked, wood-shingled roofs. The rooms of the house were plaster-finished on walls and ceilings, the plaster held in place by finger-sized poles nailed to the adzed-flat log walls. The plaster was thick, a sort of clay, painted white and falling onto the board floor in places by the time I remember first seeing it. The house had a basement; outside was a falling-in, open well. Fields surrounded the buildings.

The elevators are still dead. I'll wait a few more minutes.

SATURDAY

February 7, 1970

A round trip between New York and London to inspect our [Pan American World Airways] recently inaugurated 747 operation gives me some time to continue this letter. I expect to fly over and back on the same plane. We took off at 19:00 [7:00 P.M.]. I expect to be back in New York shortly after noon tomorrow, after a 3½-hour turn-around time in London. ⊕ *I finally had to break down the door between the elevator hall and the Trade Department last December and go down a fire escape to get out of the building. I didn't have any luck hitting the door with my shoulder, so I had to back off and run and kick it with a boot—over twenty times! For about ten strikes it looked as though the lock wasn't going to break and then a crack developed.* ⊕ *I didn't like to do a break-and-entry job, but the thought of possibly having to stay in that hall for two nights and a day before the elevators started running gave me a lot of encouragement.*

WHEN THE ROUTINE of farming was not too pressing, I sometimes blasted the larger rocks in the fields using sticks of dynamite bought from Martin Engstrom and fuses lit by a match. Thompson and I constructed a stoneboat of split oak logs bolted together. We carried and rolled the rock fragments onto this and then hauled them to a rock pile with the tractor, like a sled.

I bought the blocks for a forty-foot-high, hollow tile silo, but stopped farming before it was erected. These blocks arrived in a freight car that was left on a siding near the station. I hauled them to the farm in a wagon. During one trip, a thunderstorm drifted overhead while I was driving my team of horses along a road paralleling the railroad tracks. A bolt of lightning struck the tracks about thirty feet away, knocking the horses to their knees. I felt the shock but not at all seriously. The horses jumped up and started to gallop, but I had little difficulty holding them in check with the reins and getting them calmed down again.

Although the silo was never erected, I dug the circular trench for its foundation south of and next to the barn. In digging this trench, another of those incidents occurred which are a part of the hazards of farm life (although less serious than it might at first appear).

It was summer and I was close to seven feet down with the trench. I had decided to dig down seven feet to be sure of getting below the frost level. The walls of the trench were above my head, and suddenly the inner wall caved in, burying me to a level about waist-high and pinning the shovel down. I was concerned that an additional cave-in might bury me still farther, and that the outer wall in that area of looser earth might cave in too. Even if both walls had caved in, my head would have been clear, but how long it would have taken for someone to find me there was an uncertain factor. However, no more caving in took place, and I managed to work the shovel free and dig myself out of the earth.

Probably the most dangerous incident I encountered while farming took place on the old log building western forty. I was plowing with the tractor and had started to turn at the northern end of a furrow, having tripped the mechanism to raise the plowshares. Suddenly I saw a portion of the plow flash past about six inches from my head and thud heavily onto the ground. The lift mechanism had somehow jammed, causing the entire plow to turn over. If I had not been in a turn, the plow would have struck me almost squarely.

During one winter, I think it was the last winter that I farmed, I used the garage as a stable for two ponies. I used them to draw a light wagon and even more as saddle ponies when the roads were impassable for a motor vehicle. I bought the ponies together at an auction on a farm about two days' drive south of Little Falls. I also bought the light wagon with them and drove them back myself, stopping overnight at a farm that I came to in the evening. The stronger of the two ponies, Queen, was unbroken to a saddle when I bought her. It took me weeks to break her, using my father's western saddle—the one he had used while riding with my mother when they were living in the first house. Queen never got over bucking on occasion, but she was tireless. Prince, the other pony, was older, gentler, and not in as good physical condition.

I often rode these ponies in winter in connection with my agency for the Empire milker. Sometimes the rides were long and cold. On one of them I got caught in a blizzard at night, riding back from the area of Pierz. I lost Prince as a result of this ride—I did not realize how fatigued he had become, although I walked much of the way through the snow leading him. (I have described this trip in *The Spirit of St. Louis.*)

Storms of one kind or another punctuate my memory of the farm and areas around it: the blizzards of winter swirling snow against my face; the violent thunderstorms of summer with their lightning flashes and ear-splitting cracks and the sheet lightning making luminous demon forms of clouds. There were hailstorms, too, in one of which the ice stones were literally the size of hen eggs. I stood on the house porch and watched this storm. (I have never seen another like it.) Several half-grown buck sheep were in the driveway in front of me. One of the big hailstones landed on the head of one of them, and he acted as though another buck had rammed him.

Some of the white cedar fence posts my father had put in around 1901 or 1902 soon after he bought the land had rotted off at the base by the time I started farming. I replaced most of them with split and seasoned white oak posts painted with tar at the ground end. To replace others I used hollow, galvanized iron posts which I usually set in concrete. I experimented with reinforced concrete posts that I poured in a mold I had bought, but they were not satisfactory, breaking easily with a push after they were set in the ground. I think the sand I used in making them was too full of pebbles and not sharp enough.

I was fascinated, as was my father, with the potential uses for concrete construction, but I found little opportunity to experiment with it. One of my experiments was the small concrete pond southwest of the house in an area that I had fenced for raising ducks. I tried to make the sides slope in such a way that the freezing of water in winter would not crack them and so that small ducklings could climb out in summer regardless of the water level. As I recall, I built this pond in 1919. I scratched the date in a concrete side and with it the name of my dog, Wahgoosh. I named the pond the "Moo Pond," because I had been told that "moo" was the Chippewa Indian word for dirt, and I knew that a duck pond would almost always be dirty. This name, too, I scratched in the concrete. Unlike my concrete fence posts, the construction of the Moo Pond was highly successful. It was popular with the ducks and seems in perfect condition today—over a half century after construction.

MOO POND, the duck pond constructed of concrete by Charles in 1919, survived the onslaught of souvenir hunters to the Lindbergh farm following his successful transatlantic flight in 1927, probably because it was hidden beneath leaves.

CHARLES (left) with a basket full of lambs in the spring of 1918, and (below, left) on his Excelsior motorcycle in June 1921

One of our busiest periods on the farm came during the lambing season. A number of our western ranch sheep turned out to be poor mothers. I would walk around the farm each day, sometimes in snow and sleet, looking for abandoned newborn lambs. When I found one, I would carry it back to the house, where my mother gave it cow's milk from a bottle. Later I would take it back to the ewe and try to get her to accept it.

I attended several auction sales on farms in Morrison County. At these I bought two or three cows, some pigs, and a few farm tools, besides the two ponies. I was attending one of these auctions on the day the armistice was announced [November 11, 1918].

Although the armistice had been expected for some weeks, it raised major questions in regard to my future. My dreams of being a scout pilot were replaced by the less romantic choice between another year of farming or college. I loved farming in spite of the hard work and long hours, and I thoroughly disliked school. I decided to devote another year to farming and thereafter enter college.

About this time I bought a motorcycle, a twin-cylinder Excelsior, again through Martin Engstrom's hardware. I used it in promoting my milking-machine agency, visiting one farmer after another day after day. My idea was to build up the agency and then turn it over to someone else before I went to college. The motorcycle gave me cheap and effective transportation. I loved its power and speed and soon became a skillful rider.

In 1919 I turned the farm over to tenants again in preparation for going away to college. It was a difficult and rather heartbreaking procedure, giving up the stock and machinery and seeing my methods and hopes give way to the methods and hopes of others. But it gave me more time to spend on the milking-machine agency. This agency was disappointing in the end. There wasn't enough demand for milking machines to make them attractive from a business standpoint. Farmers were interested, but the cost of a milking machine was high in relation to their incomes. Some were afraid that it would reduce their yields of milk and eventually damage their cows.

I spent a good deal of time selecting the college I wanted to enter and finally chose the University of Wisconsin—probably more because of its nearby lakes than because of its high engineering standards. Then, as now, I could not be happy living long away from water. In the fall of 1920 I rode my Excelsior motorcycle from the farm to Madison, Wisconsin, and entered the college of mechanical engineering. That ended all my close contacts with our farm.

WHILE A STUDENT at the University of Wisconsin at Madison, Charles stretched out and leafed through a photograph album.

I returned on several occasions, both in winter and summer, but never for many days at a time. I recall one visit [1921] when I stayed alone in the house and was practicing quick draws with my Colt .45 automatic. My imagination became a bit too realistic, and I shot a hole through the kitchen-hallway door—well centered, but at too high a level to support my pride of marksmanship. (I had made both the rifle and pistol teams in college.) And after buying my first plane in Georgia in the spring of 1923, I barnstormed west to Texas and then north to Little Falls, landing near the old log buildings on the western forty of our farm. Daniel Thompson was there to meet me, ax slung over his shoulder in the manner so familiar to me in the past, tremendously impressed by my airplane, and impressed still more by the fact that I was flying it.

I felt nostalgia then if I ever felt it in my life, for I knew the farming days I loved so much were over. I had made my choice. I loved still more to fly.

CHARLES'S "JENNY" after the crackup at Glencoe, Minnesota, during his father's 1923 campaign

IN AUGUST, 1927, Charles Lindbergh received a hero's welcome from Minnesota Governor Theodore Christianson (left) and Little Falls Mayor Austin L. Grimes when he returned to his hometown with the *Spirit of St. Louis*.

THE *SPIRIT OF ST. LOUIS* on display in Little Falls during Lindbergh's return in 1927

EVANGELINE AND CHARLES Lindbergh on the grounds of the Lindbergh House during the 1927 visit

After a few days on the farm, I barnstormed southward with my "Jenny" through southern Minnesota,* Wisconsin, and Illinois to Missouri. I returned to Minneapolis later that year (1923) to take at Fort Snelling the entrance examinations for the army's flying cadet schools, which I entered at Brooks Field, Texas, in the spring of 1924.

This about concludes the information I can give you about the farm and the area around it. This letter is long enough both in time of writing and in pages. So here I will end.

---

*On his 1923 trip to Minnesota, Charles also used his plane to provide transportation for his father, who was at that time a candidate for the United States Senate. The plane cracked up near Glencoe and had to be repaired. Meanwhile primary election day passed and the elder Lindbergh was defeated.

Berg, A. Scott. *Lindbergh*. New York: G. P. Putnam's Sons, 1998.

Gill, Brendan. *Lindbergh Alone*. New York: Harcourt Brace Jovanovich, 1977. Reprint, Borealis Books. St. Paul: Minnesota Historical Society Press, 2002.

Larson, Bruce L. *Lindbergh of Minnesota: A Political Biography*. Foreword by Charles A. Lindbergh, Jr. New York: Harcourt Brace Jovanovich, 1973. A life of Charles A. Lindbergh, Sr., a U.S. congress-man and the father of the aviator.

Lindbergh, Anne Morrow. *Bring Me a Unicorn: Diaries and Letters of Anne Morrow Lindbergh, 1922–1928*. New York: Harcourt Brace Jovanovich, 1972. Autobiographical writings about her early life by the wife of the aviator, whom he married in 1929.

_____. *Hour of Gold, Hour of Lead: Diaries and Letters of Anne Morrow Lindbergh, 1929–1932*. New York: Harcourt Brace Jovanovich, 1973.

Lindbergh, Charles A. *Autobiography of Values*. New York: Harcourt Brace Jovanovich, 1978.

_____. *Of Flight and Life*. New York: Charles Scribner's Sons, 1948.

_____. *The Spirit of St. Louis*. New York: Charles Scribner's Sons, 1953. Reprint, with an introduction by Reeve Lindbergh. Borealis Books. St. Paul: Minnesota Historical Society Press, 1993.

_____. *The Wartime Journals of Charles A. Lindbergh*. New York: Harcourt Brace Jovanovich, 1970.

_____. *"We": The Famous Flier's Own Story of His Life and His Transatlantic Flight, Together with His Views on the Future of Aviation*. New York: G. P. Putnam's Sons, 1927.

Lindbergh, Reeve. *The Names of the Mountains: A Novel*. New York: Simon & Schuster, 1992. A fictionalized narrative of the lives of the aviator and his wife by their youngest child.

_____. *No More Words: A Journal of My Mother, Anne Morrow Lindbergh*. New York: Simon & Schuster, 2001.

_____. *Under a Wing: A Memoir*. New York: Simon & Schuster, 1998.

Milton, Joyce. *Loss of Eden: A Biography of Charles and Anne Morrow Lindbergh*. New York: Harper-Collins, 1993.

Westfall, Donald H. *Charles A. Lindbergh House*. Minnesota Historic Sites Pamphlet Series. St. Paul: Minnesota Historical Society Press, 1994. An illustrated guide to the aviator's boyhood home, located in Charles A. Lindbergh State Park, Little Falls, Minnesota, and operated by the Minnesota Historical Society as a historic site open to the public.

FOR YOUNG READERS:

Davis, Lucile. *Charles Lindbergh: A Photo-Illustrated Biography.* Photo-Illustrated Biographies. Mankato, Minn.: Bridgestone Books, 1999.

Giblin, James Cross. *Charles A. Lindbergh: A Human Hero.* New York: Clarion Books, 1997.

Lindbergh, Charles A. *The Boyhood Diary of Charles Lindbergh, 1913–1916: Early Adventures of the Famous Aviator.* Ed. Megan O'Hara. Diaries, Letters, and Memoirs series. Mankato, Minn.: Blue Earth Books, 2001. An account based on Lindbergh's original diary in the Minnesota Historical Society collections.

Lindbergh, Reeve. *A View from the Air: Charles Lindbergh's Earth and Sky.* Photographs by Richard Brown. New York: Viking, 1992.

Photographs and other illustrations used in this book appear through the courtesy of the sources listed below. The name of the photographer, when known, is given in parentheses, as is additional information about the item.

Reeve Lindbergh: page ix

Library of Congress: page 23 (photograph by Frances Benjamin Johnston, LOT 9791 (H) [P&P], Frances Benjamin Johnston Collection)

Minnesota Historical Society, St. Paul: pages vi (Alan Ominsky), vii (Charles A. Lindbergh album, ca. 1915–1922), 3 (toy airplane likely made by Lindbergh as a boy or by his father or by both of them together; Charles A. Lindbergh House collection, Little Falls, Minn.), 4, 5 (Nelson), 6, 9 (David B. Edmonston, Washington, D.C.), 16 (Solem Studio), 17 *left* (A. P. Overland), 17 *right*, 18, 19 (album, ca. 1915–1922), 20, 21, 22 & 26 & 27 (all in Charles A. Lindbergh and Family Papers), 28 & 30 & 32 & 33 (all in album, ca. 1915–1922), 35, 36 (photograph courtesy of Minnesota National Guard), 37 (album, ca. 1915–1922), 40 *top* (from *Farm Implements* [Minneapolis], May 31, 1917, p. 27), 40 *bottom* (from *Farm Implements,* July 31, 1917, p. 7), 41 *top* (album, ca. 1915–1922), 41 *bottom,* 46 (album, ca. 1915–1922), 51, 52 & 53 (all in album, ca. 1915–1922), 54 *top* (Charles A. Lindbergh album, 1923–1924), 54–55 *bottom,* 55 *top,* 56

Lindbergh Picture Collection, Manuscripts and Archives, Yale University Library: pages ii (Lindbergh rafting on the Mississippi River near Little Falls, about 1912), iii (detail) & 1 (Lindbergh in the cockpit of the *Spirit of St. Louis,* May, 1927), x (Lindbergh in St. Louis, Missouri, at the conclusion of his tour of Latin America with the *Spirit of St. Louis,* February 1928), 12

Printed in the USA
CPSIA information can be obtained
at www.ICGtesting.com
JSHW052019140824
68134JS00027B/2557

9 780873 514224